All the Best

Characters

50 drawings by Joan Worth

From the Wallflowers Series – Volume #5

ISBN-13: 978-1725853386
ISBN-10: 1725853388

All the Best Characters * from the Wallflowers Series #5 ©2018 Joan Worth

All the Best Characters * from the Wallflowers Series #5 ©2018 Joan Worth

All the Best Characters * from the Wallflowers Series #5 ©2018 Joan Worth

All the Best Characters * from the Wallflowers Series #5 ©2018 Joan Worth

All the Best Characters * from the Wallflowers Series #5 ©2018 Joan Worth

All the Best Characters * from the Wallflowers Series #5 ©2018 Joan Worth

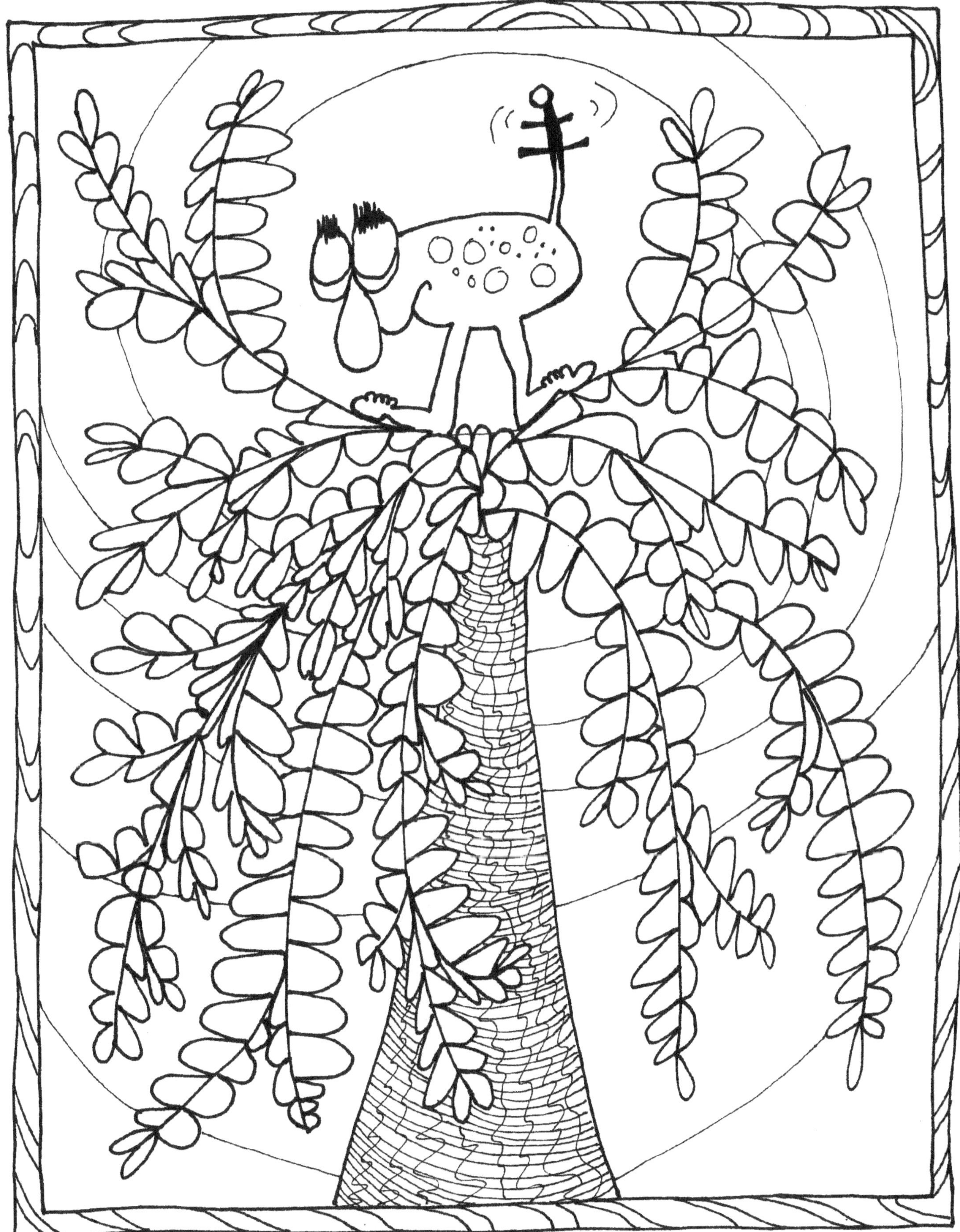

All the Best Characters * from the Wallflowers Series #5 ©2018 Joan Worth

All the Best Characters * from the Wallflowers Series #5 ©2018 Joan Worth

All the Best Characters * from the Wallflowers Series #5 ©2018 Joan Worth

All the Best Characters * from the Wallflowers Series #5 ©2018 Joan Worth

All the Best Characters ✳ from the Wallflowers Series #5 ©2018 Joan Worth

All the Best Characters * from the Wallflowers Series #5 ©2018 Joan Worth

All the Best Characters * from the Wallflowers Series #5 ©2018 Joan Worth

All the Best Characters * from the Wallflowers Series #5 ©2018 Joan Worth

All the Best Characters * from the Wallflowers Series #5 ©2018 Joan Worth

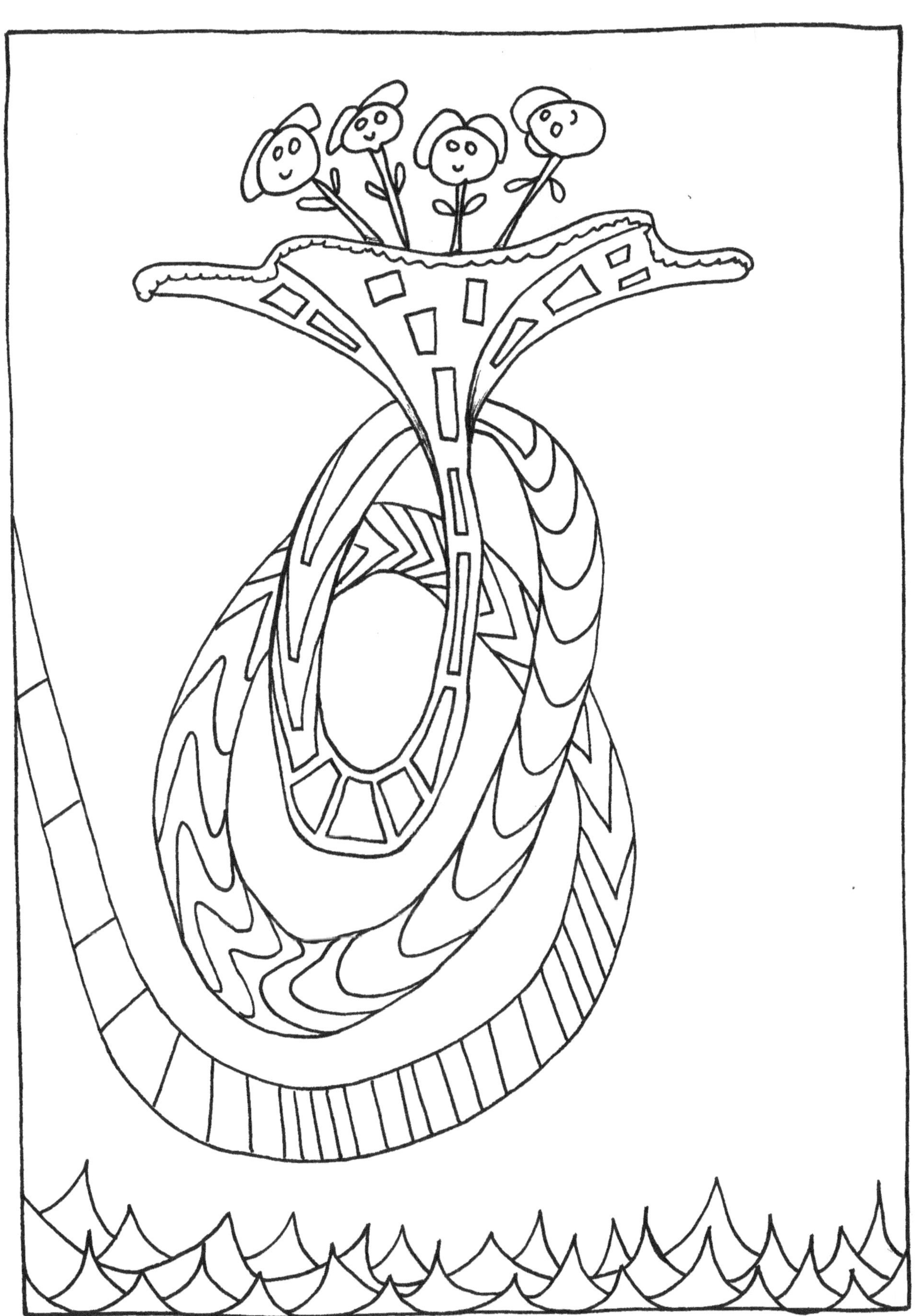

All the Best Characters * from the Wallflowers Series #5 ©2018 Joan Worth

All the Best Characters * from the Wallflowers Series #5 ©2018 Joan Worth

All the Best Characters * from the Wallflowers Series #5 ©2018 Joan Worth

All the Best Characters * from the Wallflowers Series #5 ©2018 Joan Worth

All the Best Characters * from the Wallflowers Series #5 ©2018 Joan Worth

All images taken from the
Wallflowers Series

Wallflowers Volume #1
Pages 1-23
Wallflowers #2 volume #2
Pages 24-36
Pick Me Volume #3
Pages 37-50

All the Best Characters * from the Wallflowers Series #5 ©2018 Joan Worth

www.ingramcontent.com/pod-product-compliance
Lightning Source LLC
Chambersburg PA
CBHW080028260726
48658CB00007B/2519